Y0-CAZ-617

The Clapp Memorial Library
P.O. Box 627
Belchertown MA 01007

DISCARD

Extreme Encounters

BLACKBIRCH PRESS

An imprint of Thomson Gale, a part of The Thomson Corporation

Detroit • New York • San Francisco • San Diego • New Haven, Conn. • Waterville, Maine • London • Munich

© 2005 Thomson Gale, a part of The Thomson Corporation.

Thomson and Star Logo are trademarks and Gale and Blackbirch Press are
registered trademarks used herein under license.

For more information, contact
Blackbirch Press
27500 Drake Rd.
Farmington Hills, MI 48331-3535
Or you can visit our Internet site at http://www.gale.com

ALL RIGHTS RESERVED
No part of this work covered by the copyright hereon may be reproduced or used in any
form or by any means—graphic, electronic, or mechanical, including photocopying, recording,
taping, Web distribution or information storage retrieval systems—without the written
permission of the publisher.

Every effort has been made to trace the owners of copyrighted material.

Photo credits: cover, pages all © Discovery Communications, Inc. except for pages 5, 8, 13, 19,
30, 35, 38–39 © Photos.com

Discovery Communications, Discovery Communications logo, TLC (The Learning Channel), TLC
(The Learning Channel) logo, Animal Planet, and the Animal Planet logo are trademarks of
Discovery Communications Inc., used under license.

LIBRARY OF CONGRESS CATALOGING-IN-PUBLICATION DATA

Extreme encounters / John Woodward, book editor.
    p. cm. — (The Jeff Corwin experience)
    Includes bibliographical references (p.).
    ISBN 1-4103-0228-8 (hardcover : alk. paper) — ISBN 1-4103-0229-6 (pbk. : alk. paper)
    1. Animals—Juvenile literature. 2. Dangerous animals—Juvenile literature. I. Corwin,
Jeff. II. Woodward, John. III. Series.

    QL49.E934 2004
    590—dc22
                                        2004004482

Printed in the United States
10 9 8 7 6 5 4 3 2 1

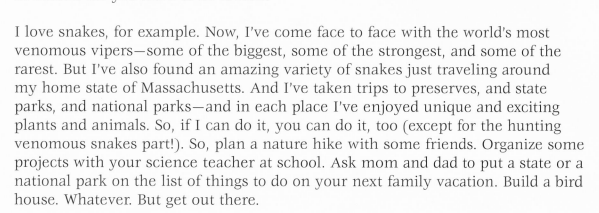

Ever since I was a kid, I dreamed about traveling around the world, visiting exotic places, and seeing all kinds of incredible animals. And now, guess what? That's exactly what I get to do!

Yes, I am incredibly lucky. But, you don't have to have your own television show on Animal Planet to go off and explore the natural world around you. I mean, I travel to Madagascar and the Amazon and all kinds of really cool places—but I don't need to go that far to see amazing wildlife up close. In fact, I can find thousands of incredible critters right here, in my own backyard—or in my neighbor's yard (he does get kind of upset when he finds me crawling around in the bushes, though). The point is, no matter where you are, there's fantastic stuff to see in nature. All you have to do is look.

I love snakes, for example. Now, I've come face to face with the world's most venomous vipers—some of the biggest, some of the strongest, and some of the rarest. But I've also found an amazing variety of snakes just traveling around my home state of Massachusetts. And I've taken trips to preserves, and state parks, and national parks—and in each place I've enjoyed unique and exciting plants and animals. So, if I can do it, you can do it, too (except for the hunting venomous snakes part!). So, plan a nature hike with some friends. Organize some projects with your science teacher at school. Ask mom and dad to put a state or a national park on the list of things to do on your next family vacation. Build a bird house. Whatever. But get out there.

As you read through these pages and look at the photos, you'll probably see how jazzed I get when I come face to face with beautiful animals. That's good. I want you to feel that excitement. And I want you to remember that—even if you don't have your own TV show—you can still experience the awesome beauty of nature almost anywhere you go—any day of the week. I only hope that I can help bring that awesome power and beauty a little closer to you. Enjoy!

Best Wishes!
Jeff

Extreme Encounter

I'm Jeff Corwin. You probably think I'm in some exotic place, as usual. But you're wrong! I'm actually at home.

I'm Jeff Corwin.
Welcome to Extreme Encounters.

That's my house ... where I prep for each big adventure.

Home for me is a small island off the coast of New England. Here, surrounded by a lot of friendly creatures in the safety of my own home, I'd like to share with you a collection of my most extreme encounters from around the world. We're going to look at some of the extreme wildlife encounters we've had. These are the biggest, the baddest, the strangest animals we've seen: the extreme encounters.

First up—the baddest. On the island of Komodo, I wasn't looking for a friendly greeting, since these animals are called dragons. This is the place where we're going to find Komodo

Like the time I was on the island of Komodo.

dragons. They can be up in the hills or in forested areas. You can even find them on the beach. We are definitely in Komodo country. Look at this guy right here. This big dragon is definitely on the trail of something. There's another one moving right over there, and he's picked up some sort of scent trail. His tongue is moving. He smells something.

Look at that ... Komodo chaos!

The strongest dragon gets the best part.

Teeth like this are nothing to mess with.

Something very big is happening over here, a lot of chaos. This is a perfect example of how powerful these creatures are. They're carnivores, they're predators, and they illustrate that in what they're doing right now. These guys have a goat, and it is shredded. The strongest individual Komodo dragon has first access to the kill, and it basically trickles on down to the smallest one. They are just pulling it apart. An animal that might have weighed a hundred pounds or more will be devoured within minutes! It feels very dangerous to be this close to them. Words can't convey the sound of bones crunching and flesh tearing.

Komodo is an extreme place. But Bali is a paradise: green, tropical and rich in culture. It's also home to a very scary serpent. I trekked up into the mountains with a local snake guide named Astori. Even though we were looking for a snake that had a reputation for being aggressive, nobody knew just how dangerous this afternoon's stroll would be.

Bali is a tropical paradise.

The Komodo dragon is a fearsome and powerful predator.

I really want to catch that king cobra.

He's extended that beautiful hood...

and he's looking right at me.

There it is! My most favorite cobra is the king cobra. I'm trying to assess the situation. I really want to catch this creature, but it is a very venomous animal. I'm a little nervous. And my footing on this wet, slippery rock isn't helping.

He's now in defensive posture. He's got that beautiful hood extended. He's looking right at me, eye to eye. This is a huge king cobra—absolutely magnificent. They call this creature the king of the serpents because he won't flee like many other snakes. And his diet consists of snake. He is a snake eater. Astori tells me that you're supposed to just to stand there, let him rise up to you, and then sweep your hand around and grab him by the back of the head.

I don't know if I've got enough gumption to do that, so Astori will show me how to freehand capture a king cobra. Astori grabs the king cobra by the tail so it won't slide down the stream. The snake has his mouth wide open just before Astori secures him. Talk about extreme! This whole encounter was an in-your-face reminder of how careful you have to be when working with a potentially dangerous animal.

Isn't he beautiful? It's a regal, handsome snake. Look at that face. I just want to secure him—not too loose, not too tight. You can see he's been shedding his skin. He is pushing 9 feet in length. He is a good-sized and very powerful snake. This snake will certainly defend itself, and it does so with extremely toxic venom. Just holding this king cobra is a thrill I'll never forget.

Then there was that time in Borneo...

Look at that!

Let's see—dragons, king cobras—how about something else extreme? How about a herd of very wild elephants I found in the jungles of Borneo? Researcher Burt Dausip and I were tracking this herd the entire morning, but we had no idea we would even see the elephants, let alone be able to get close to them. As it turned out, we got too close.

We're surrounded by elephants. It's amazing to me that an animal so gigantic can move so quickly through this brush and be so agile. These very intelligent creatures are using their extremely loud vocalization. They're trumpeting to establish territory. They want us to know they're here. It's their warning.

This was a group of adolescents—teenagers out looking for trouble—and they found us. Burt and I thought we found a path that would take us away from the elephants, but the trail went right back to the main herd where the babies were.

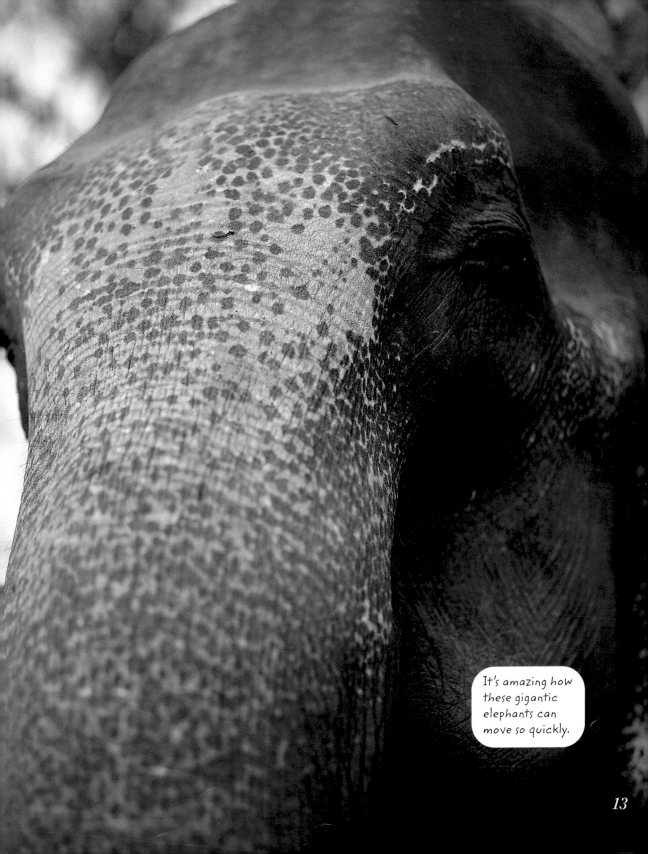

It's amazing how these gigantic elephants can move so quickly.

13

A whole herd of elephants.

We've got a lot of noise here because these are adults with babies. They're in a defensive line and they're very angry. At this point, we are in danger, but you have to hold your ground. If the elephants sense any fear, they're going to use that to their advantage. Hold your ground, but be ready to run if you have to. At this point, it's definitely time to make a hasty retreat. Burt and I find a narrow escape route just in time.

Even though it's summertime, and I'm at home with the ocean beckoning me to go fishing and raspberries begging me to be picked, I've got work to do. I'm prepping for my next big adventure, and speaking of big, check this guy out. It's an albino Burmese python. In the wild you'd never see one this color. You might see one this size, though. I use this guy for lectures on natural history to teach people about snakes. But in the wild, I've seen snakes like this. This guy's 10 feet long, but I've seen them twice this size.

Just hanging out at home with my big friend…

an albino Burmese python.

Here are some of the biggest creatures I've found. Thailand is filled with big animals, both elephants and cats, but I wanted to find a member of the longest species of serpent on the planet. Underneath this blanket of water hyacinth is a very large reptile that I want to grab before it grabs me. Where are you, Mr. Snake? I have to watch the head because this snake can deliver a very potent bite. Here's his head. This is a reticulated python. It is the longest snake in the world. There are records of this animal reach-

This reticulated python lives in Thailand.

It's the longest snake in the world.

ing well over 30 feet in length. This individual is probably about 10 feet long. What he's showing us is his mode of both defense and taking down his prey. He is a constrictor. He squeezes the breath and life out of the creatures it's going to eat. This is a good time to let this reticulated python go and say thanks to this great reptile for providing us with a great wildlife experience here in Thailand.

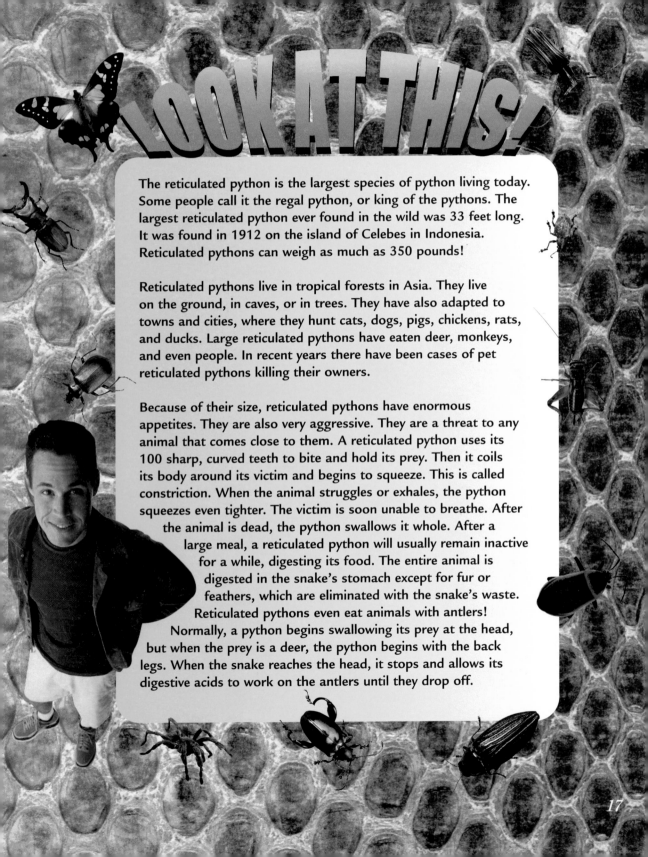

LOOK AT THIS!

The reticulated python is the largest species of python living today. Some people call it the regal python, or king of the pythons. The largest reticulated python ever found in the wild was 33 feet long. It was found in 1912 on the island of Celebes in Indonesia. Reticulated pythons can weigh as much as 350 pounds!

Reticulated pythons live in tropical forests in Asia. They live on the ground, in caves, or in trees. They have also adapted to towns and cities, where they hunt cats, dogs, pigs, chickens, rats, and ducks. Large reticulated pythons have eaten deer, monkeys, and even people. In recent years there have been cases of pet reticulated pythons killing their owners.

Because of their size, reticulated pythons have enormous appetites. They are also very aggressive. They are a threat to any animal that comes close to them. A reticulated python uses its 100 sharp, curved teeth to bite and hold its prey. Then it coils its body around its victim and begins to squeeze. This is called constriction. When the animal struggles or exhales, the python squeezes even tighter. The victim is soon unable to breathe. After the animal is dead, the python swallows it whole. After a large meal, a reticulated python will usually remain inactive for a while, digesting its food. The entire animal is digested in the snake's stomach except for fur or feathers, which are eliminated with the snake's waste. Reticulated pythons even eat animals with antlers! Normally, a python begins swallowing its prey at the head, but when the prey is a deer, the python begins with the back legs. When the snake reaches the head, it stops and allows its digestive acids to work on the antlers until they drop off.

I can't believe I'm holding the world's largest species of scorpion.

What a freaky arachnid!

There are giants all over the jungles of Borneo, including this big black arachnid. Look at the size of those claws! This is really a once-in-a-life-time chance to hold the largest species of scorpion. He's huge and freaky! And look at the size of those claws, and that stinger! Scorpions belong to the group of invertebrates we call arachnids.

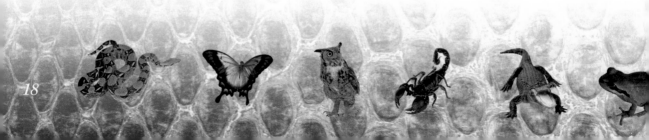

Check out the size of his claws and stinger.

He's got two body segments—the one in the front with the claws, and the one in the back where the stinger is. A very close relative of the spider, these guys are excellent hunters. He uses his claws to hold his prey, and he's got a very poisonous stinger. I've worked with a lot of scorpions and this is the biggest one I've ever seen in the wild. He is huge! I've had enough. He's creeping me out, so I'm going to let him go. We'll find a good place to put him before he crawls up on my shirt.

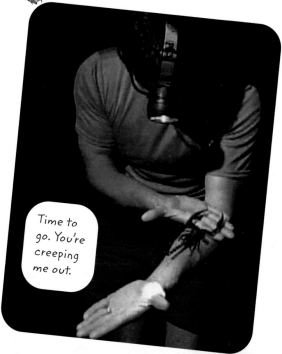

Time to go. You're creeping me out.

Does this Malayan fruit bat have an adorable face or what?

Here's another creature that gives people nightmares—giant bats. I've studied bats all over the world, and these are absolutely the biggest flying mammals that I've ever seen. I love bats, and this is one of my favorites. It's a gigantic bat—the world's largest species of bat, the Malayan fruit bat. He's very different from the bats I've studied in Central and South America because this bat has excellent vision. He uses his vision and his wonderful sense of smell to find his food. And in the case of this species, it's fruit.

Hey, look. I'm Batman!

I'm just going to fix your wing here.

Its wingspan is almost 5 feet.

Now you're wondering, how did Jeff Corwin just walk in the woods and grab a wild bat? Well, this isn't a truly wild bat. This is a rehabilitated bat that now lives in captivity. I wanted to show him to you because it's just extraordinary to see this creature. It is a flying mammal with a wingspan of up to 5 feet or more. You don't have to be a bat mother to find this creature adorable. In fact, its muzzle is very caninelike, hence the name flying fox. Keep in mind that this animal has no relationship to canines. This creature is pure bat, despite its puppy dog complexion.

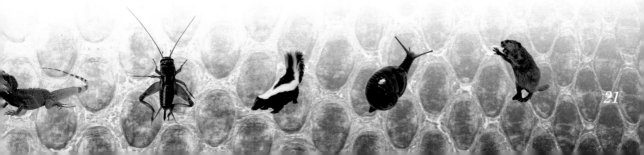

Scattered throughout this dense thicket of mangrove are hundreds and hundreds of Malayan fruit bats. Their chirps and the shrill calls are overpowering my ears right now. Some of these individuals have nearly a 6 foot wingspan, and they fly beautifully. These guys can go up to 40 miles in a single night to look for food. They hang out here during the daytime hours, and at night, they detach from the branches, open their wings and take flight in search of food.

This guy's got major muscles.

As long as we're talking about big things, take a look at the size of this frog. That's his defense—he's got pectoral muscles. He could pop a cap off of a soda bottle. See those spines in his chest? That means it's mating season. *Leptodactylus pentadactylus*—very surreal. I've never seen one this big. He's been eating bats, he's been eating fish. These are cool frogs.

Have you ever seen a frog this big?

See that cute canine in my window?

That's my little Teacup.

Now I'll show you some of the smallest animals. Here in my bedroom is something I want you to see. This is Teacup. Isn't she the most precious thing? Teacup is a fennec fox, one of the smallest species of canine in the world. She's cute, but she's tough. She likes my wife, she likes me, and she gets along with the cats. She attacks everyone else. She's a wild animal. In order to have one in captivity, you have to have a legitimate reason. I have a permit, and I use her for lectures and education. But we love her. She's only 3 pounds.

It's fun to cuddle with a fennec fox.

Don't let that sweet face fool you.

We call her Teacup because when she was a baby, she could fit in a teacup! She's a reminder that great things can come in little packages.

Teacup's a wild animal.

Come on. I'll even carry you across.

My search for some of the smallest creatures ran into a snag in Thailand. The water was running high, and I had to carry my 5-foot-tall guide across the river! I already showed you the largest bat in Indonesia, and now I want to show you the world's smallest.

I have to be so careful, because this is a very fragile mammal. I have just netted the smallest flying mammal

I have to be very careful.

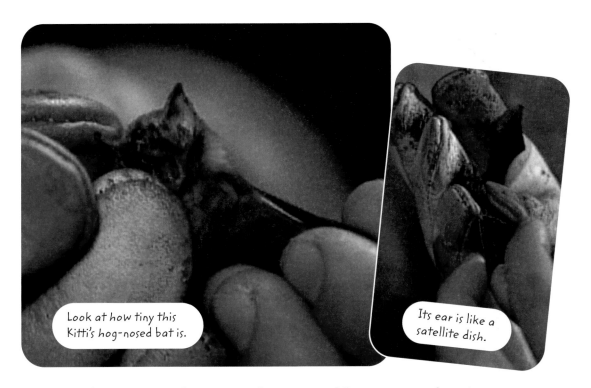

Look at how tiny this Kitti's hog-nosed bat is.

Its ear is like a satellite dish.

on the planet. It is the Kitti's hog-nosed bat. From the tip of one wing to the other, it is only about 4 inches. It's only a couple of inches from the tip of its nose to the tip of its tail, and it weighs about 2.5 to 3 grams. This is a tiny, delicate creature. Those ears are like satellite dishes. They use them to receive the sounds that it screams out into the night sky. Some scientists believe that they use these sound waves to create an image of their environment. So with sound, he's almost seeing me, who he perceives as a potential predator.

I've got the world's smallest chameleon right here!

It's hard to walk with those skinny stick legs.

I wonder how long it would take that tiny bat to fly to Madagascar? Here, we can see the smallest chameleon in the world. What a fantastic creature! I feel like I'm looking at a Muppet, some sort of puppet created by a human being. But in fact, this is a living, breathing chameleon. This is *Brugesia minima*, the smallest species of chameleon in the world. Typically you find this lizard no more than 2 or 3 feet above the forest floor. They like to stay low to the leaf litter. He's not a fantastic climber. His body is much bigger than his limbs are. They are just twiglike.

Chameleons are famous for their ability to change color. They can change into a variety of colors, including blue, yellow, green red, black, or white.

Many people believe that chameleons change color to match the color of their surroundings, but this is not true. Chameleons actually use color to communicate with others. A chameleon might take on the color black, for example, when it is angry or defensive. It might become red and yellow when it is interested in mating.

Chameleons are such interesting creatures that many people want to keep them as pets. Sometimes this leads to problems. In 1972, the owner of an Oahu, Hawaii, pet store imported dozens of Jackson's chameleons from their native Africa to sell as pets. When the shipment arrived, the animals seemed tired and weak, so the owner let them out in his backyard to help them recover from the stress of travel.

A single Jackson's chameleon can produce up to thirty-five babies every six months, so their population grew rapidly. Today, they have spread to the islands of Oahu, Maui, Hawaii, and Kauai. Jackson's chameleons use their long sticky tongue to capture insects. Since they are an alien species in Hawaii, they have no natural predators there. This means there will be more and more chameleons and less and less native Hawaiian insects. Native Hawaiian insectivores, such as birds, will have less to eat, and their populations might decline. Chameleons are fascinating creatures, but they should be left where they naturally live.

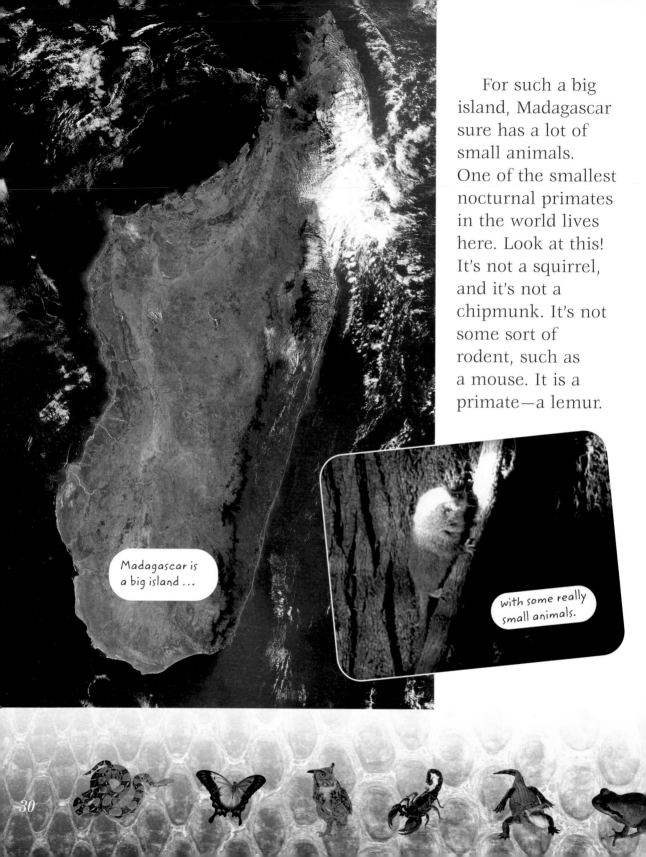

For such a big island, Madagascar sure has a lot of small animals. One of the smallest nocturnal primates in the world lives here. Look at this! It's not a squirrel, and it's not a chipmunk. It's not some sort of rodent, such as a mouse. It is a primate—a lemur.

Madagascar is a big island ...

with some really small animals.

This is the brown mouse lemur. He's a cavity dweller. He wants to be protected inside a hole. In the daytime hours this is where you find them—in a hole. So he's taken the palm of my hand as security. We human beings have a distant genetic relationship to these animals. When you look at this creature and see those little fingers, those eyes looking at you curiously, perhaps wondering what is going to happen to it, you can't help but feel compassion for it. I wonder what the future holds for this wonderful thing, as well as the other animals that have evolved so magnificently, so bizarrely, so wonderfully in this island called Madagascar.

We found that huge, muscle-bound frog in Panama. I also found one of the smallest I've ever seen there, too—the tiny, beautiful poison dart frog. I never had a tougher time trying to catch a frog in my life. This is one of the smallest species of denderbates, or poison dart frogs, living in the Americas. But they have an excellent defense. They manufacture a deadly toxin in their skin. When this venom enters the blood stream of a predator, the predator usually dies. But there's something else that's amazing.

This poison dart frog is carrying tadpoles on his back.

This is the male, and he's transporting tadpoles on his back. His back is bubbling with life, the new generation of poison dart frogs. Some species will move those little tadpoles onto their backs and take them to good locations for them to grow up in, such as the funnel of a bromeliad. This is something to remember.

I'm babysitting this precious tiger cub.

I don't think she wants to play with the serval cub.

This is Niki, one of our three pet cats. And this precious baby right here is certainly not a pet. It's a wild animal—a three-week-old Siberian tiger cub. I'm just babysitting. It belongs to a zoo and we're just helping to rear this baby.

This here is a serval, another wild cat. It loves to play. It's another guy we're just taking care of in our house. What's great about our world is that it's filled with wonderful cats. And cats have provided me with many of my most memorable encounters.

The serval is one of our world's wonderful wildcats.

35

I met these Buddhist monks in Thailand.

Look at him playing with that tiger!

In Thailand, I was a little nervous at first. This place is one of those hidden treasures you won't find in travel books. It is a Buddhist monastery that doubles as a tiger haven. So here are a bunch of guys in robes and sandals running around and playing with these tigers! It's incredible!

Playtime always ends too soon.

Boy, he's got a lot of guts to grab a tiger by the tail! They're just one big happy family here. These tigers were freed from inhumane captivity or orphaned by poachers. They are unable to live in the wild, so they will spend the rest of their lives here at the monastery.

This guy looks hungry.

Hey! Don't look at me.

Tigers can be deadly predators.

Well, playtime is over. It is time to head back to the main building where the tigers sleep and are fed. I asked the monks how they are so comfortable being around such powerful, sometimes dangerous predators. They told me that the tigers trust them, so they trust the tigers. I didn't trust this tiger as much as the monks did, but I have to tell you that it was an amazing afternoon. This was easily one of my most memorable experiences.

Whether in Thailand or Namibia, big cats are some of the most awe-inspiring animals on the planet. At first, these guys were a little difficult to spot. Get it? Spot? It's a cheetah! If you let your eyes scan this landscape quickly, you don't see anything. But hidden in the grass are some very powerful, amazing carni-vores. Cheetahs can almost magi-cally disappear into their habitat because they have beautiful cam-ouflage. They are built for speed. Their heads are low to the ground. Their backs are slightly arched, and their feet stretch out like running shoes. They can run at speeds of up to 60 miles an hour to take down their prey. I don't recommend facing down a wild cheetah by clapping your hands at them, but this time it worked.

Now those are the teeth of a true carnivore.

Built for speed ...

We'll get to Madagascar in a minute, but first lets stop in Ecuador to find one of the strangest creatures you'll ever see. Look at this cricket! It's got huge antennae. It's a female. You can see that by the long shaft coming off the back end of its abdomen. That's the ovi depositor. That's where it lays its eggs. But what's amazing about this thing is the way it looks. I feel like I should be in the movie *Men in Black* or something! It's like an alien. It's an extraordinary creature.

Madagascar has some weird looking crickets.

I feel like I'm holding an alien.

We're eye to eye with an aye-aye!

For my money, Madagascar has the strangest animals on the planet. Now we're looking at one of the most mysterious of all lemurs. It's the aye-aye. I have always wanted to see an aye-aye. I would love to see one in the wild, but they're nocturnal. They spend much of their lives up in the canopy. They are extremely hard to find, very secretive and very reclusive. He's using his incisors to sculpt a hole inside the egg. Now he's using his fingers to dig it out. This is a very, very unusual creature.

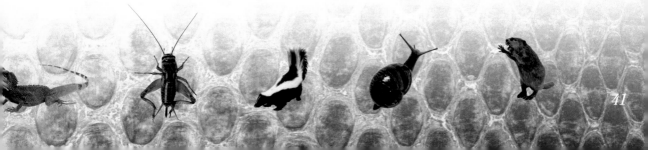

This handsome creature is one of Madagascar's many chameleons.

He's puffing up his chin to scare us.

There are sixty-five species of chameleons on the island of Madagascar, each one stranger than the one before it. This is the *Furcifer pardalis* chameleon. Not only is this one of the largest of the chameleons in Madagascar, but he can make himself even larger. He's feeling a little threatened, and he doesn't know what to make of us. He wants us to think that he's big and bad, and he does that by extending his chin like a pouch and puffing up with air. He's also displaying bright, bright colors. He looks fierce. He hopes he looks too big to tango with. I told you that Madagascar has the strangest creatures!

Sorry, buddy. You're not that tough.

If you let your eyes scan this bundle of leaves, you'll discover that one of these leaves is not like the others. This is a katydid. It's a grasshopper-type creature, an herbivore. He's so leaflike that he actually has the venation of a leaf. If you look very closely you can see the central vein going down the middle with all the small little veins radiating off of that. Perhaps you might look at it and think he's got some sort of disease. This demonstrates how amazing evolution is. He's not diseased. He's a very healthy insect. But his skin, or his exoskeleton, is crunched up. It looks dried and frayed, as if it is a dying leaf. A predator would think that this little creature is nothing but a leaf. Let's put this little critter back.

Looks like a leaf with legs, but it's a katydid.

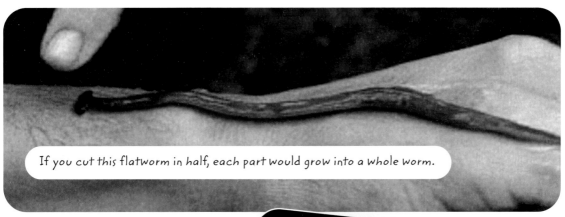

If you cut this flatworm in half, each part would grow into a whole worm.

Here's a flatworm. Something that's neat about this creature is that it can reproduce both sexually and asexually. How does that happen? Well, if you cut this guy down the middle, you wouldn't kill him. You might wound him, but both separate pieces would then regenerate their own separate body parts and create two individuals. It's amazing.

Do you like my mustache?

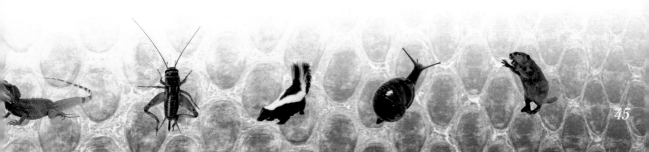

Before you go, meet my favorite snake...this beautiful Western hognose.

Unfortunately, our adventure, this *Jeff Corwin Extreme Encounters*, has to come to an end. I hope you had a great time. I'm going to end on a good note by showing you my most favorite snake. I've had this guy since I was a kid. It's a beautiful Western hognose snake. But our time's over for now. I look forward to seeing you on our next Jeff Corwin Experience in this wonderful world of ours.

Glossary

albino an animal without pigmentation, or coloring

arachnid a type of invertebrate, such as a spider or scorpion

camouflage coloring that helps an animal blend in with its environment

canine related to the dog family

carnivores meat eaters

chameleon a type of lizard that can change the color of its skin

cobra a hooded, venomous snake

constrictor a snake that squeezes its prey to death

invertebrates animals without a spinal column

mammal a warm-blooded animal that gives birth to live babies and feeds them with milk

pectoral muscles upper chest muscles

poachers people who illegally hunt animals, especially endangered ones

predators animals that kill and eat other animals

primate a type of mammal such as monkeys, apes, or humans

reptile a cold-blooded, usually egg-laying animal such as a snake or lizard

serpent snake

toxic poisonous

venomous having a gland that produces poison for self-defense or hunting

Index